Celestial Descent

(Second Edition)

Poetry for and from the Soul

Kiran Sandhu

A dedication to the eternal spirit that exists as the universal oneness and man's quest to realize the divine truth.

Preface

John Keats, one of the most famous English poets of all times wrote that "if *poetry does not come naturally as leaves to a tree, it had better not come at all."* Let me at the outset proclaim that poetry did not indeed come naturally to me. Consider this, having lived in this world for nearly half a century, I have never written poetry as such before. Just some very vague scribbles from a material mind nothing much to look at. Thereby I am of the firm conviction that the words that fell like tear drops on the paper and took a poetic expression are not mine. I was perhaps just a medium to hold the pen while the flow came from a source beyond!

When the flow started I had no clue that the literary sojourn over the last six months would culminate into a collection of verses worthy of sharing with the readers. But somewhere midway I became present to the call of getting the work published and sharing it with fellow beings who might be interested in a genre of this nature. And while the poetic journey was on way, the raven dropped by asking me to add a bit of artistic touch in the form of drawings to accompany each poetic flower in the bouquet. So the same have been added herein and the reader may interpret both the poetic and art expressions in their own ways but the message underpinning the book, I beg must not be lost. To state it in more clear terms, the poetry unravels the musings of the forlorn human soul and takes one to the journey where both the creator and the created merge as the oneness that exists in its myriad forms in this world and beyond. The book is divided into four sections but all linked by the common thread of the oneness that runs through them. The first section *'Divine Encounters'* is presented in the form of

i

an encounter with some of the spiritual Avatars that walked the earth. The second section 'Nature's *Musings*' recites spiritual melodies sung by natural forms. The third section *'Revered Touch'* brings to fore a soul's understanding and comprehending the eternal truths of life. The last section *'The oneness'* bridges the divides that are so intrinsic to us humans and merges all that exists into the ocean of divine oneness.

And if you, the reader are holding this book, then believe that your journey has begun, to a path beyond the self. Pray, let me gently hold your hand and lead you to walk across the bridge and then leave you at your own horizon to discover and hear your own musings and soul rumblings. May your journey be enriching!

CONTENTS

Divine Encounters 1

    Tea with the Buddha...3

    Walking with Guru Nanak................................7

    The Flute Player 11

    A Discourse with Rumi 15

    Thus Spoke the Son of God.............................19

    All Paths Lead to Thee 23

Nature's Musings..26

    The Cosmic Dilemma....................................28

    Springs Blossoms 31

    Night, The Enchantress 35

    Wails of the Wind...39

    Wave on the Ocean 42

    Nature's Sermon 45

Revered Touch 48

    Ode to the Breath..50

    Ode to Love 54

    Soulmates 58

    The Joy of Sorrow 61

    Sensual Intoxication 64

    The Invisible Chains......................................68

    Ode to Death..71

The Oneness 74

    The Oneness of it All.....................................76

The Dance of Life...79

Existential Predicament 82

Creator's Lament 85

A Devil's Mourning 89

Thou Indiscernible One 93

Like a Rudderless Boat...96

Miracles 99

Divine Encounters

'I was lost in the maze on a heap of quicksand
When in stepped thee and took my hand
Walk with me child, I have something to tell
And so I went with him and on his words did I dwell'

Tea with the Buddha

Tea with the Buddha

It's was a beautiful starry night
And the moon shone so bright
As I gazed outside my bedside window
Sleep descended gently as I hit the pillow
Drifting into a magical world of dreams
Who would I meet tonight, my soul excitedly pondered
And lo behold, I saw a magnificent vision
A spark of his halo, his footsteps I ran to follow
And as he stopped and turned towards me
His radiant face lit by a subtle smile I see
In recognition and reverence I bowed to thee
It was the Buddha himself visiting me.

Oh wondrous lord where have you been all these years
Eons have passed in wait and in tears
But now that you are here
There's nothing else that I care
Please sit down with me and have a tea
I know your time is precious but I have questions for thee
Queries, alright he said but I shall answer only three
So sat down the Buddha on the floor next to me
Only three, why that not enough
The task you have given me is rather tough
For life cannot be condensed in just three questions
But since you ask, I shall attempt an inquisition.

So as the Buddha sipped on the tea
I began my voyage into the raging sea
Of human mind and answers it can't find
And he, the lord himself must answer to me

Who am I my lord, why was I born
Why is it that I feel so forlorn
What then is the purpose of my life
Answer me oh Buddha, the self realized
His deep oceanic eyes dwelled on my persona
As if gently chiding me for my dilemma
You my child are not the first
To feel the hollowness or the thirst.

Thousands of decades ago when on this earth I wondered
For answers of the unknown I fell and stumbled
Till enlightenment was bestowed on me
My soul was fulfilled and I felt complete
Though your spiritual sojourn is totally your own flight
Let me show you just a bit of light
You are a fragment of the divines own soul
Born you were with an earthen form to reach a certain goal
Forlorn you feel because your direction is lost
Your human purpose was to realize the eternal ghost
As he stood up with a sigh and looked me in the eye
I felt the guilt of having so far lived a lie.

Sensing my desperation, Buddha held me in his embrace
It's never too late my loved one, you can still retrace
Adore me in your heart as you do me on your shelves
My statues you put everywhere but for my wisdom also you must care
As I wept in solace and held his hand
Said he, I know you wish I would not leave
But I have tasks and many promises to keep
To awaken humans from their deep slumber
I must travel in time and in their dreams I wonder
Maybe a spark shall ignite deep under

As we bade goodbye, I knew something had changed

As I gently opened my eyes at dawn

The imprints were there though the Buddha was gone

Was it a dream or a reality

And then I saw that empty cup of tea

Sitting on the table, giving me a subtle glance

Of the night that passed, a surreal reminiscence.

Walking with Guru Nanak

Walking with Guru Nanak

The hills behind my abode are dressed in autumn hues

Colours orange and crimson, before set in the winter blues

A strange longing rises as if by a mystical design

So I take my being for a stroll under the canopy of shades nine

As I walk in the forest heart further and further

A gravitational force pulls to which I surrender

The wind that blows on that setting ball of fire

Blows a faint melody to my ears as if played from a lyre.

As I hasten towards the melodic strains

Two humanly figures I guess from their gaits

Must be shepherds I try and presume

Playing the lyre and its soulful tune

The distance fades and facing the other we stand

Two saintly men, one with a rubab in his hand

It wasn't the lyre but the Rubab's musical strands

Guru Nanak and Mardana, they sure do look exact

How can that be, it's been centuries since they left

My senses don't believe but my heart says it's him

The one that I have turned to when my days were grim.

And behold he's here, in his heavenly avatar

My salutations I offer and beg for a favor

Can I walk some distance with you lord

If that's not too much to ask

You can my child but ask me not where we shall go

Ask me nothing for there's nothing you already don't know

Let the path be my choice and if you agree so

Walk by my side and together we can go

With a quiver in my heart and turmoil in my mind

I walk by his side but keep looking behind
As if an illusion was fading in time
Below our feet it's a cloud I swear
How spectacular is this heavenly stair.

Not a word is uttered but the rubab joyfully sings
Weaving a magical spell, heavenly bliss it brings
The animals and the birds, rushing to their nests
Stop to listen to the musical quest
Each note speaks directly to the heart
Mardana he's so adept with his Rubab
The Guru then sings his verses aloud
The trees sway and so do the clouds
Such a heavenly baritone of a saintly bard
Its pierces the sky and the rocky mountain heart
The message it reveals is that we already know
But buried deep inside till light gives it a glow.

The light of his song brings life to my soul
Realize the truth and make that your goal
Rudderless we walk through our limited earthy time
How profound and simple is the message sublime
And as I realize what my being already knows
I turn around to the Guru to thank him so
For the walk of wisdom and diving in the depth
Of divine knowledge and spiritual quest
But as I turn around, I suddenly hit the ground
The physical form of the Guru who was here with me
I look all directions but still fail to see
Desperate I call and my heart sadly wails
Was it real or my mind spun delusionary tales.

So I retrace my footsteps and walk through the forest

Taking the same trail from where we did start

My vision falls on the ground and my heart does pound

Three pair of foot prints embedded on the leafy mound

Tell their own tale, of the Holy Grail

For that evening I took a holy walk in the clouds

The Guru himself dispelled all my doubts

Now whenever I walk amongst the trees

I try to catch that faint melody with my ears

The rubab with its magical notes divine

Are forever etched on the sands of time

Carrying an timeless message of living and dying

So walk with Guru Nanak, the eternal wisdom shall be thine.

The Flute Player

The Flute Player

Its late in the evening, the cows are heading home

By the banks of River Teesta, I sit on a wet stone

I'm here for an intent and I must that recall

Before the night descends, the curtain should fall

On my life and end all that I have lived so far

Perhaps I may be forgiven and become a shining star

I have nothing else left but to come to you

Oh almighty let this wish be true

So thinking this I spoke to the swirling waters

 Embrace me in this last journey, deliver me to the master

As I got up to dive in the dusk coloured river

Goodbye my loved ones, I depart forever

And then I looked around and rested the final gaze.

The forest greens seemed draped in a misty haze

The life there around making hummable sounds

A cacophony in harmony from the birds home bound

But amidst all that, a strain that bound the symphony

A melody so rapturous it stopped me in my tracks

An irresistible urge seemed to pull me back

Into the forest I followed the trail

Spellbound and pushed by an invisible gale

Perched on the branch of the old banyan that grew

His colour of twilight and dark shades of blue

Smilingly, he looked down at me

Pray why so sad my lass, said he.

As I looked up bewildered

At the head with a peacock crown

Is it you lord Krishna, I made a shaky sound

Me it is dear and I know all that you fear
Nothing is hidden and let me say this
You are running away child and you shall on life miss
How can there be pleasure without pain
Affection without disdain
Love without hate, calm without spate
Can there be happiness without sadness
Laughter without sorrow, today without tomorrow
Joy without tears, courage without fears
Sun without the moon, morning without the noon
Mountains without plains, losses without gains
Day without the night, peace without the fight
Roses without thorns, adoration without scorn
A jump without a fall, a big without a small.

And if you ask me I could go on and on
But is this not enough to show you not to mourn
Whoever said life and living would be always charming
Even if you see its duality, it is all but one
A beautiful concoction for you to take on
And if you drink it well, I must tell you so
The diamond shall be polished, the amber shall glow
For that is your life my child, please know
Play your part best and then merrily go
When I call upon you, my flute will tell you so.

Until then play the game and play it you must
You will write a beautiful chapter of life, I trust
As I woke up from the trance, the notes had faded away
Night had descended and my head did sway
Could this be true, I thought for a moment or two
The darkness draped forest but a light had shone through

Lighting up my heart as had never happened before
What a magnificent gift this life, with all that it holds in store
And now when I walk along the Teesta, my endearing mate
The distant flute still sings to the river in spate
Marking a surreal presence in all that is there
Encompassing the universe in a huge magical choir.

A Discourse with Rumi

A Discourse with Rumi

It was a cold dark moonless night

The wind howled in pain as I heard its plight

The rain fell against my window pane, as if begging to let her in

In the warmth of the room, where I lay on my bed

A book of verse sat on my lap which I read

The poems are soulful but I don't understand

If only the poet could help me comprehend

The deep meanings and interpretations

That could remove my misconceptions

If only I could find the depth of the lines

If only the magical poetic verse, could with me converse

If someone could enlighten my ignorant mind

I shall be forever grateful to thine.

As I wishfully looked towards the scene outside

A face on the window caught my eye

An old man drenched to the core

With folded hands he gestured, open the door.

Let me in my dear one I heard him say

that's my verse that you are reading I pray

Puzzled I unlatched the door

Rumi! In amazement I could utter no more

How can that be you, you left centuries ago

Am I dreaming or you are real, please tell me so.

A gentle smile played on his lips

It doesn't matter or not whether I exist

Time for queries alas there is none

There is a lot in there but the message just one

All that you see in this vast universe

is the forms of the one as I state in my verse
The one that we all seek is in you my son
Go deep inside and you shall find that divine one
The Mecca, the temple and the church my friend
is within you where your pilgrimage shall end

Infinite treasure shall itself reveal
Glorious bounties for the soul to heal
Arrogance and pride brings doom I say
With faith and devotion to the one you must pray
So let go of the illogical logic, it's an obstacle
In the path of divine miracles
Your limited intelligence is yet another hurdle
It causes you to mistrust and stumble.

Your material attachments bind you to lust and greed
Let go all vices and be free I plead
Your egoistic self is yet the biggest vice
Discard it forever, don't be a novice
For once your soul is washed pure
Your life's goal will be achieved, that I am sure
So I say this in a Sufi way, in his shadow you must ever stay
In each heart beat remember his presence
The giver of life and its beautiful expressions
With love and compassion, for self and all
Bliss you shall find and that's not all
The divinity shall enrich your very soul.

As tears of realization rolled down my eyes
The great Rumi embraced me as I woefully cried
Oh holy one, what favour have you done
To come and speak the truth with this one who is but none

With what can I thank thee

for bestowing enlightenment upon me

The rain had stopped and but not my tears

As I gazed upon his face divine to see

I knew he tore away a part of me

The part that was myself, now forever gone

Instead a new one had birthed with identity none.

Smiling he walked away into the dark night

But lifting away my darkness and bringing in light

As I often now ponder, of that night I wonder

But when I open my book of verse I see

His name in black ink that he wrote for me

His verse or himself, it does not matter

But it changed my life for the better

Oh Blessed Rumi, may you ever live

May your verses and poems forever give

What you gave me was the gift of the truth so sacred

May all mankind be bestowed with your divine knowledge.

Thus Spoke the Son of God

Thus Spoke the Son of God

Its Christmas time yet again

And that wonderful nostalgic feeling

Seeps into the warm heart, its numerous hues revealing

And even though its windy and freezing

The winter snow falls slyly teasing

There is something in the cool surge of air

A bonhomie that permeates everywhere

My breath becomes an amazed sigh

As I gape up to the wondrous night sky

Shimmering through its twinkling eyes

There is one that stands outrightly bright

Is that the sacred star of Bethlehem

I marvel as I look starry eyed

Yes it is, I hear a tender voice

The one had led the three wise men that night

Eons ago to witness and to sight

The miraculous birth from a virgin mother

There has never been or will be another

I am that one born, holy father's blessed son

Jesus they call me, redeemer of all, foes I have none

Dazed I turned around, from where had come the sound

From the snowy mist as if descending from a living dream

A most radiant face, the gentlest eyes that ever could have been

But what was that a crown of thorns around his head

And blood still seeping from the wounds, I looked in dread

Centuries had passed without healing his nail struck chest

And wait what's on his back that he drags along

Damn me, it's the wooden cross they had hung him on

Why has he not removed it still carrying as if it belongs
Like a limb stitched to him but a heavy burden within.

Sire I beg you to let it go, a sorrowful happening that occurred long ago
And that forsaken crown that burrows deep into your furrows
Sucking blood like a thorny wicked leach
Pray my lord, tell me what is it that you come here to preach
His eyes turn moist and sad, he said hear my dear lad
This burden of burdens is forced on me
I had come to the world to save mankind and thee
From his very own demonic lower self
I thought his inner devils would die
Drowning in the tears of remorse from his eyes.

So I gave myself happily that he could live well
But centuries have passed and I have this to tell
You see this crown with red droplets streaming down
Is the blood of my mother earth and the innocent burnt in hearth
And the cross that I must carry, is the weight of his sins so many
Alas, the Satan has won and I must bear the burden
For eons on and on until he mends his ways
And for that he must, his inner dragons slay.

Till then my cross and thorny crown, I shall not put down
Christmas, it may well come and go
My unhappiness shall remain ever so
For what is the point of celebrating my birth
If he does not imbibe even an iota's worth
Of divinity and the path divine for which life I gave mine
Then carrying his burden the Lord walked into the haze
Leaving me to wonder in a complete daze
And as my numbed heart felt an ache so strong

I stood rooted to the spot but the vision was long gone.

Wild hallucination, said my devilish mind
But the soul knew the truth and it wasn't at all kind
And as hot tears burnt a hole in the snow
It revealed a rosary with a cross below
From within the ground, a treasure so profound
To remind ignorant mankind of the one beyond time
To resolve to crucify the evil within we must try
For Son of God to be freed do this we must
Remove the impurities and all that's ego's dust
Revered Christmas, you will come every year around
Redeem we must so the true spirit resounds.

All Paths Lead to Thee

All Paths Lead to Thee

Those early hours of dawn, that day when I was born

Into the world I came, to play life's game

And to play my part I must be someone they said

That someone must bear a mark for which they care

Enough to give up their life and I too must join the fight

So I was baptised, blessed and with a name dressed

Which made me a religious entity, with a label and identity

I looked up in despair and said to my creator

Listen to me sire, this was not of my desire

I did wish to descend and in that transcend

The karma of previous lives and my incomplete strides

To you the divine master to be with you ever after

But my lord what is this a mesh of unseen chains

I see the dark waters and I feel the pain.

Said my lord the divine, your anguish is genuine

But I must clarify that which you religion call

Was meant to spiritually align one and all

As higher human beings of divnity

To be in sync with the cosmic order of my creativity

And so I sent the avatars to the world

To spread my message of oneness of all

For each human to know that within them I lie

For which they must light the spiritual flame and fly

Christ my son, he spread the message of love

Even for those who crucified, nailing him to the cross.

Buddha, the wise one was sent to show

The path of enlightenment that you all must know

Krishna the spiritual mentor he came

To steer you towards the true name

Mohammed the prophet, he asked for complete surrender

Of your false identity and self, to silence your egoistic inner chatter

Nanak my loved one, he walked in all directions

To show you the path of devotion and compassion

No Hindu and no musalmaan he conveyed my sayings so strong

That all of you are one but I must tell you what went wrong

The Bible the Gita, Guru Granth Sahib or the Koran

Call them whatever you may but the path to oneness is one.

But you humans did me a great disservice

Scorned my messages and indulged in false practices

Created segregated religions if I may use that term

Made false interpretations and caused so much harm

Spread hatred and vile in place of universal love

In my name you don't hesitate to spill the other's blood

Religion if you call it was meant to be a path

Of righteous life and selfless love for all.

Whatever religious path you took would shatter

Your ignorant self and lead to me so how did it matter

You garnered false identities to the hilt

A Hindu or a Muslim a Christian or a Sikh

And forgot that you are a bit of me the divine

My creation, so you all are mine

All paths eventually lead to me

If you follow any righteously

So remove the labels and burn the ego

Your religion is oneness, all others you must forego.

My heavenly father, said I, take me with you let me die

Release me from the human form I beg and cry

My child you must stay and must you then convey

To the world what I have had to say

You have the wisdom and you should stay

Tell them all paths lead to me

Live in brotherhood and then see

Higher spiritual flights towards the eternal light

And when time comes return to my heavenly sight.

Nature's Musings

'Nature you are such a good teacher
If only I had eyes to see and ears to hear
Your tales would then be seen and heard
And many secrets would you happily share.'

The Cosmic Dilemma

The Cosmic Dilemma

As the golden sun lights up the horizon
The earth and the sky dance in a cosmic union
Like two lovers in an evergreen romance
Caressing the other, with every chance
The sky, like a king woos his earthen queen
Who wears a gown of gold and green
Awaken, my beloved for the sun is here
Fill my thirsty heart with your soulful stare
My king, the sky, my knight in shining armour
For you, such love struck feelings I harbour
For I am nothing without your loving embrace.
You are the benefactor of my sweet succour and solace.

To all our beautiful children who live upon my crest
The humans, the animals, the trees and the rest
You send down the air that moves everywhere
The breath of life for them to thrive
And the ball of fire that glows in you
It warms their hearts, bringing smiles anew
And the rain that fills my rivers and springs
Brings the precious nectar for our dear offsprings
And when they are tired, you bring in the blanket
Of the star studded night, whose darkness delights
Oh my beloved sky if it was not for your affection
My heart would turn cold and would cease my existence.

My beloved queen earth, thus spoke the sky
You give me the reason to live, let me tell you why
You have showered your love on me, all through the eons
Much pain you have borne and given birth to my children

You fed them and nourished them from your own breast
Embracing them in motherhood you gave them the best
You held them by the fingers and helped them to grow
To turn them to divine beings good seeds did you sow
But alas my love, I'm much saddened to say this
Your eldest one the human, has caused us much anguish.

For his mother earth he does'nt at all heed
His eyes see only that what he needs
In his greed he has made you bleed
Causing terrible wounds and bruises upon your being
My sad eyes cry when this I am seeing
To his other siblings, the animals and the greens
He has been so ruthless and has brought them screams
He murders and plunders for his never ending lust
He has poisoned you my dear, reducing you to filth and dust
I tell you we were better off without this treacherous child
I wish I had the means to take away his life.

No my king, said the earth in tears
My child loves me not but I am the mother
How can I disown the one from my womb
With my own hands how can I ever create his tomb
Do as he may but he shall realize soon
What he does is bringing him terrible doom
When this happens, he shall deeply repent
And I, the mother, shall embrace his lament
So dear sky, look me in the eye
Give him his time and till then let's pray
That our human child does not go further astray
He returns to his senses and lives in peace ever after
With his mother, the earth and sky, the father.

Spring Blossoms

Springs Blossoms

Oh extensive winter, you unleashed you turmoil and ferocity

Our earthen home you bound in a frosty snowy tapestry

But hail the sun after a long hiatus its journey has again begun

Playing hide and seek from within the clouds

Its golden arrows pierce the earth's frayed shroud

Melting the snows, warming its brown weathered breasts

Spreading a thrill to the flora, whom the chill had mercilessly undressed

Baring them so ruthlessly, stripping them of their modesty.

Winter you are so cruel like a haggard old witch

Who said her spells and darkness she stitched

Of shades embroidered in black and grey

The brightness she consumed and brought dismay

But all that will now be undone

The angel we waited for has finally come

With a enchanted wand and a healing potion

She prepares a therapeutic connotation

And hey presto, begins the magic conjuration.

The enchantress conjures up a radical transformation

My love, the earth you must be dressed in my wardrobe's best

And I must bring varying shades of rich green

To don your bosom and make you a queen

The trees they croon as they sway and swoon

Dress us up oh beloved spring

Let our blossoms birth and bloom

So she flies up to the radiant blue sky

Plucking colours from the rainbow

And then to the moon and stars that glow

The silver and the gold

She grinds fine in a turquoise mould
Till a glitter is reaped, which she then gathers in a heap.

But wait, another flight is to the golden ball of fire
To him she tells her heart's desire
Begging him for gold spun threads to sew her beloved's attire
And when the arduous task ends
She takes a dive and gently descends
Weaving a green veil slow, the earth's bridal trousseau
Preparing grounds for romance
Of the love struck hearts that joyfully dance
And as they lie on the velvet green beds
Spring your loving demeanor spreads
As they call her out, she asks them to be
And starts to drape the excited trees
Sprouting their buds, birthing infant leaves
Painting them with such deft but delicate ease.

The glitter that she spun from the celestial ones
Now adores the bodies of her joyous daughters and sons
But the task so beautiful one may ask, is to paint the blossoms in varied hues
The trees, shrubs and bushes, in the colours they choose
Tender shoots and buds as they sprout on bare wooden arms
Smile a radiant smile as of lovers in a trance
Flowers so heavenly as they bloom
Completely lift away the winter gloom
Innumerable the colour and shades of spring
Oh what joy our redeemer brings.

When the furious winter tore away our robes
Baring us and striking us with its bone chilling snows
We waited in hope and in despair

When shall we hear our beloved spring's choir

How reverently we prayed for iciness chains to break

Nothing seemed right, our life was at stake

But the mist has lifted and hence returned the time

You have dressed us in your finest designs

To laugh , sing and dance in a blissful reverie

With sun kissed rays and cool breeze romancing the trees

Forgetting their frost bites and wintry scars

Spring it heals and it does so fast

And as they say, what they have to say

Always and forever bear in your mind

If winter comes, can spring be far behind!

Night, The Enchantress

Night, The Enchantress

I have lived the long day and gone through its fray

Working through tedious routines

Almost like a human machine

Fast life in the city lane

Takes its toll and it drains

Me of my peace and it's a daily chain

How I wait for the seductress

To ease my aches with its soft caress

Each dusk she arrives dressed in a velvet black negligee

Embellished with the stars and moon, a lovers true fantasy.

She smiles at me a sensual smile

Her glossy lips give me a gentle kiss

How enchanting is her seductive dance

It holds me in a wondrous deep trance

I am intoxicated by her charismatic charm

Lovingly, she pulls me in her arms

And rests my head, on her delicate breast

If I could drown, I would choose her eyes

With the depth of the ocean and expanse of the sky

And as she begins to sing her sonnet of true love

Heavens descend on the ground from the skies above

As I lie in her magical embrace, her gentle hands stroke my face.

My hurting heart throbs with a deep longing

I need to find that sense of belonging

So I touch her long tresses and look in her eyes

Take me to the moon and the star studded skies

Make love to me, I murmur softly in her ear

For the pain of separation I can no longer bear

So she tenderly yields and her satin carcasses

Spread over me and takes over my senses

And as she engulfs my being, time stops still

I am in another world, where all is tranquil

Such is her feel of love and compassion

My heart wells up with love and admiration

Oh lady Night, you are such an enchantress.

The haughty Day has much to learn from your prowess.

Day, you arrogantly shine bright but with the suns light

Human Hearts you torment and the creatures lament

You make them toil, never resting a while

You push hard and you grill

And grind their souls in the material mill

But night she brings such solace and succour

I forget your harsh ways and rejoice in her slumber

Human, forgive me but this I must say

You are the ones that define me, the day.

You run and you race and you want to ace

Blame me if you want, but it's surely not right

I am just like my twin sister, the charming night

Like her, I want you to have fun and frolic

So I light up the space with the sun's magic

But you have no time to stop and see

To admire the daylight, landscape and the humming bees

So wrapped you are in societal traps

You consume the day in all that's crap

And then colour me with guilt, come on that's not fair

See me in my true colours, just slow down and stare.

The grief of the Day pulls at my heartstrings

For once I stop in my tracks, looking around at things

The pristine blue sky, the snow capped distant mountains

The lush green glowing valley and rippling water fountains

The chirruping in the bushes, the squirrel and their antics

The flowers that brush against my apparel

With angelic cheer they nod and dazzle

All these years of daylight, how much have I missed

Stuck up in my quarry mining for success

Oh Day, I say, with regret so true

With deep melancholy, shedding a tear or two

Indeed your lament is precise

If night is so precious and exquisite

Your worth is no less, you are the cause of many a delight.

If night is an enchantress, you are to say the least

A sunshine princess that creates a heavenly feast

For the senses to rejuvenate and rejoice

Alas, it's us humans who create a dismal premise

For the creator who made you in his own mystical ways

Did not discriminate between his daughters, the night and day

Our human lives, we walk through your crust

Till then we must relish your each moment with faith and trust

Till time brings us to our muddy dust

And we take an eternal heavenly flight

Forever to be one with your oneness, oh divine Day and Night.

Wails of the Wind

Wails of the Wind

Know me I am the wind, nature's own prodigious child

In my different avatars I exist, from extreme harsh to mild

See me you cannot but you can feel and hear

When I touch you so daintily or my callous self causes a scare

When I softly whisper or screech in a violent ire

You can feel my mighty presence even in the nothingness that you stare

I am the air the elixir of your living story

From your first breath to the last, I am your faithful ally

I am your silhouette, I never let you down

Until death does us part, I remain in foreground.

When you fall in love, I become the tender seductive gust

So young lovers romance on my unseen crust

Exchange sweet nothings and love's idyllic musings

I play lullaby's turning into a breeze so tender

To my tunes, your form dances so petite and slender

harmonious echo's I play from my heart's accordion

To light your soul I become the nature's proficient musician

But I'm afraid, my dark self I must also reveal

that side of me, can cause many a upheaval

For when in a fit of rage I cross all bounds

I turn into a vicious gale and with wrath I pound.

I become the monster that uproots and kills

Inebriated in my strength I tears apart hills

I dash and I smash creating wreckage in a flash

My tentacles I spread which the earthen beings dread

My violent self spares none in its ugly ferocity

When on a vengeance trail, my rampage hath no mercy

I turn into a wind storm that howls over the terrified oceans

Conjuring up colossal waves sinking ships to its dark deep bottoms.

Why I do this don't ask, for natures assigned me my tasks
For like all other beings, I also exist in duality
My soul is pure love but my ego gives me a devilish personality
But what can I do, it's the creator's divine will
I can't change my natural traits but human you can instill
For he has given you the power of judgment and reason
To be equanimous whatever the time or season
But you wear many faces like me the wind
Your dual existence is a foe not a friend

You wear your inflated egos up your sleeve
Never listening to your soul, yourself you deceive
Changing your colours like the moods of the wind
Varying shades of misery and sadness you bring
When you have the option to be like the divine
Poor wretched me can only wish and pine
Learn your lessons from the wails of the wind
Find your own true self and become nothing
For when we are nothing, we become everything
Merging with the eternal and the timeless being
Riding my crest, songs of divinity you sing
In perpetual bliss and the endless spring.

Wave on the Ocean

Wave on the Ocean

Standing on the silken sand, running a finger through my gray strand

I look at the horizon, where the ocean meets the sky

What a sight to behold, a feast for the eyes

As the sun drowns in the oceans dark depths

Its colour blue, it turns a fiery red

The lull is broken by a thunderous wave

Menacingly dancing as if in a rage

It emerges like a giant in the fading light

And strikes at the cliff with all its might

Its show of strength, here does not end

It comes fuming on the sand

And drenches me to the bones with its watery hand.

Naive human don't you know

I am the king of the ocean and this I must show

I can strip and rip all that obstructs my way

I am almighty, this with conviction I say

When I rise on a moon lit night

The tide can wreck havoc on all in sight

Do you know how the boats and the ships fear me

I can tumble and toss them over, can't you see

Many a watery grave have I made

Of sailors and ships, to rest I have laid

So don't you look me in the eye

For I can in a split second and take your life

Carrying you in my fold to the ocean deeps

Where you shall be put to eternal sleep.

Oh haughty wave, high and mighty you behave

Alas you know not the truth, so you live in falsehood

You are nothing but a wave in the ocean, very soon your time will end
When you fall down with this water, you shall blend
There is no you and it's this you must learn
You are just a bit of the ocean, into it must you return
Why then do you threaten can you learn to be humble
For your day shall come too and you shall tumble
Back into the oceans heart, you shall be a wave no more
No identity of your own you shall dissolve forever.

So my dear friend be gentle and kind
Touch me not as a foe but as a friend benign
Caress the shores and lend a helping hand
To the boats and the ships take them safely to land
Kiss the cliffs and the rocks while you are alive
Bring them cheer and in true friendship you shall thrive
For dear wave, I human am just like you
The time is short and there's so much to do
But I wile away my life in sorrow and strife.

We humans are nothing but waves on the ocean
Alive for a brief moment and then we must return
As you to the ocean, we to the eternal one
To the creator that gave us the gift divine
Of life and its beauty to experience and shine
To know the truth we must dive deep within
And you the wave must do the same
From the oceans heart shall emerge that name
Baring the truth for all to see
In the cosmic dance, you and me,
Here for a moment and then shall cease to be.

Nature's Sermon

Nature's Sermon

As I walked by the seashore one evening
The wet sands beneath my feet, shimmering
I stared blankly towards the horizon
My mind worried as restless thoughts spun
Of regrets and desires, lighting malignant fires
What I could have achieved more from life
My ambitions I could have easily materialized
And how happiness would have then touched my feet
Now I am filled with sorrow of unfulfilled dreams I cannot meet.

As I look down in grief, I hear someone speak
My friend why cry, look me down in the eye
I am the soft sand that embraces your feet
If only you could feel my grains beneath
And then spoke the gentle wave from the sea
Have you ever seen me dancing in glee
When I romance the sand and caress her strands
How amazing the feeling is, will you ever understand.

Then spoke the sea gull have you seen us gliding down
With my pretty companions, we make such joyous sounds
We sing a chorus with the sea waves
And perch on the glossy rocks and rave
Oh what a life without any care
We thank the creator for bringing us here
Then spoke the soft sea breeze
Felt me have you ever, tell me please
For when I touch with my silken hands
The waves jump in joy and so does the sand.

The forests croon in delight, the birds take long flights
Together we gather, to create a magical symphony
But notice it you might not, for you are drowning in misery
After spoke the sea turtle, the secret of my long life
I go slow and enjoy the small joys that each moment brings
In harmony I live with other beings, together we sing
Songs of nature's bounties, we have been generously granted.

If there is a heaven it is here on earth, but only if you want it
But alas my human friend you fight, for material things and ambitions futile
You fail to look at the beauty that surround you
Your fleeting happiness lasts for only a moment or two
For you rest it on material goods and gains
But egoistic pursuits bring nothing but pain
It's time to change and I must tell you so
Dear brother or else in melancholy you shall go
Stop and look at the universe around
Such wondrous creations in this world abound.
Each one created to bring you unmeasurable joy
To fill your heart with love, to soar your spirits to the sky
Drop your illusions and painful self conclusions
Detach from the quest, then you shall find the best
Much more worth then silver and gold
Is the joy of inner peace and bliss I am told
Yield to Mother Nature and ecstasy shall be yours
A remedy for all ills she has all the cures.

Sermons I had received from the sands and the dainty breeze.
The turquoise turtle, who then returned to the sea
My gloom was lifted and my heart felt so light
In a magical moment, my soul was released of its plight
As I looked around with new found eyes

Love filled my being, at the majestic sight

That feeling of union and a great communion

With all around and this I found

Was a priceless feeling, it brought a great healing

The divine himself had come in his myriad forms

To awaken from my meaningless slumber and take me home.

Revered Touch

'I wished for joy and sorrow is what I got
My world collapsed and I was so distraught
Till you with your sacred grace
Lifted me beyond and granted me solace.'

Ode to the Breath

Ode to the Breath

A soft murmur that I would rarely hear
I hardly felt it as if it wasn't there
And went about life without a care
Never stopping to stand and stare
Or wonder how I ever did exist
What kept me going, I never did ponder
Worldly desires made me dive deep yonder
As if that was all I was here for
Me, myself and all that was more
And today, as I lie on the bed
Gaping for air and my battered breath
I feel her go in and out
As if it in my ears my breath does shout.

It's me who kept you alive all these years
From the time you were in your mother's womb
I whistled softly so your heart could beat
When you were in that soft cocoon
I rocked you gently into a sound sleep
And when you were born
I breathed in you the gift of life
Through your giggles and tears
I was always there, and when you were eight
And your dad gifted you the bicycle
I rushed excitedly into your lungs
So you could cycle, with all your might
And boy, you did it day and night
How happy were you, it made me sigh in delight.

And remember that day when you first felt a stirring
Of love and emotions and all its longing
A teenager you blushed, your heart skipped a beat
And me I blowed in cool air you felt from head to feet
And when you both held hands, I looked up to your face
I felt the joy in you bursting and slowed down my pace
So I, the breath, did not come in your way
To feel the ecstasy and sensuousness
Of first love and its all encompassing happiness
And then you became that handsome young man
Who wished to rule the world and heart of every maid
And me I gave you all that I had
A breath was I and you, a young lad.

So together we ran and we ran forth and younder
Did we ever stop I cannot really remember
But now my friend, you are a sick old man
And me I am trying but no longer can
For the master of mine, he has sent a sign
So I have to stop and let you go
I have been yours for all these years
And now I must leave you with a heavy heart and tears
But as I leave you dear one remember
This last journey we shall embark on together.

Said I in panic, my breath please don't go
Stay with me forever, I love you so
But sadly as she faded away
And along with her I felt a sway
In death I realise that our breath is fixed
And what more can I say she is a divine gift
Friends and my dear loving mates

Life is all about the breaths that we unconsciously take

Lady breath is a treasure, of invaluable measure

And a reminder of our mortal self

Cherish her and live life everyday anew

For one day she shall leave and so will you.

Ode to Love

Ode to Love

Oh love, how sweet is your sweetness
All beings yearn for you
In all your forms and shades they long to be enslaved by you
The lofty mountains so high
Long to be kissed by the sky
To feel at its core, the love so pure. .

The water from the spring yearns to falls from great heights
To meet its beloved the earthen depths in delight
It's love that instills a great strength and will
To take the fall, pain stands small
Such great is the joy, beyond the sorrow and pain
That the water yearns to fall in its beloved's lap again and again.

How earnest is the graceful Gulmohar tree
 To meet its beloved, the breeze
For when it embraces, her slender trunk it holds
A great romance gently unfolds
The branches and leaves, swaying and skirting
Explode in a rapture, joyously, flirting.

In the fields where the farmers work all day
Lie waiting the shafts, for the month of may
When their beloved, the Sun shall shine so bright
And spin golden hay in its glowing light
Cheery bales shall adore the undulating heights
Warming to the embrace of their lover in ecstatic delight.

In the crimson forests, adoring the hill tops
The lissome doe dances, her frolic never stops

Calling out to her mate, the handsome Deer
Who rushes to her call, to be so near
And looking into those wide black eyes
He muzzles her velvet coat and wishfully sighs
Both chase each other and run all around
Then in gentle succor, lie on the moist ground.

Further, another, who is a darling Mother
To a little chubby boy holding tight his toy
She swoons down to hold him close to her bosom
Her face oozes love in its awestruck expressions
Of a smile or a frown, or a hiss and a kiss
Try to fathom the depths of this priceless treasure
For this form of love is beyond any measure.

How the heart zooms as a new romance blooms
The young boy and pretty girl
Their hearts take a frivolous swirl
Fall heads over heels from dizzy heights
Into the magical pool of love and its unbounded joys
Of passion and desire and soundless musical lyre
Oblivious to the world, as if only they exist
Amidst the sun, the moon, the stars, and the mist
Exchanging insatiable glance
Holding hands as they playfully prance
Somber promises of everlasting love they utter
Tunes of sweet nothings, they in a daze, mutter.

Deep in a trance, as if its his only chance
The wise Sage, his face tells it all
Of a great love thine, with who else but the divine
How radiant is he in total bliss, intoxicated with the sacred kiss

As he opens his smoldering eyes and looks to the sky

He raises his hands up and loudly sighs

If he had his way, he would discard his body today

He would leave the mortal mud and fly up to be with his beloved

In eternal spiritual form he shall transcend to the heavens above.

Oh love, you are the creator and the destroyer

You are the cradle but also the pyre

You exist in all and all exist in you

If I can't live without the valued breath

I can't even live without you

For you are the creator's most visible expression

Without you it would be all doom and destruction

For love it's the cosmos that you surround

It is you love that makes the world go round

Oh revered love, how divine is your divinity

You are the essence of all and infinity.

Soulmates

Soulmates

You and me, me and you
Soul undivided yet bodies two
Singing the songs of love
Soaring and surging high above
The warm earthen mass
Both the lad and the lass
To the distant, heavenly skies
The twin soul spread its wings and flies
On the clouds, joyfully romancing
On the rainbow, elatedly dancing.
Sliding down a thunderous raindrop
sitting on a snowy mountain top
walking through the forests green
The sun kissed grass, its blades so lean.

Caressing the chestnut and the pine trees
Feeling the breeze rustle through their leaves
Hearing the choral sounds of the jungle
With the wind stray notes that mingle
Flowing down the humming creek
The waters splash around and speak
The trees, the leaves and the passing breeze
The sky, the rain, the sun and the moon
All in one tone, a query croon
Tell us why twin hearts you beat
Tell us what is it that feels so deep
Tell us why you surge and soar
Tell us why for we must know more.

Know if you must, our allies we trust

For when we descended from heavens blue
The souls drifted apart and we became two.
One was her and the other was he
Of body and breath and the elements five
The earth, fire, air, water and the sky
Of all the parts, it was the heart
That was made of materials so fine
The fire of desire and feelings divine
With layers of emotion of love and yearning
Centered with a core of benevolence and belonging
Celestial is the rule that gives a diction
The souls that split while in heavenly creation
In their earthen gowns they must find the other.

The he and the she must come together
The twin hearts when they beat, must beat in unison.
To drown in divinity and deep devotion
To feel the depths of the ecstatic love
Surge and soar they must to the skies above
Hand in hand, in joy and in sorrow
Together in life and beyond tomorrow
And when the earthen form dissolves away
The souls shall merge, meet and twine
Becoming one with the creator divine
Floating together, on cloud nine
Never to be born, never to die
Soulmates forever, you and I.

The Joy of Sorrow

The Joy of Sorrow

Joy you are such a delusion

You are fleeting and a fluttering emotion

Humans, they pursue you with all their heart

Such arrogance, you reveal yourself in bits and parts

Everyone wants you but me they shun

They can chase you to the moon but from me they run

Your truth they know not or else they would stop

Your dependent nature on the desires that they foster

If unfulfilled the joy swiftly turns to sorrow

And hence I step in until you return perhaps, tomorrow.

They abhor me and try all means to escape my embrace

Mistaking it for a bitter thorny disgrace

But never have they tried to realize

That's it's the presence of me that gives joy its valuable space

You can't exist without me, this thought gives me solace

Like the summer and winter, autumn and spring

In the game of life happy and sad songs we sing

But value me you must and let that be sure

It's from sorrow that your soul is cleansed of the things impure.

Its sorrow that's the love potion of the divine

It's me you must drink to realize the celestial truth beyond time

While endless joy is the essence of your soul

To reach that state I must take your toll

I must astound you and ground you

Inflict you with misery and pain

It's only then you will rise to make a greater gain.

A gain so large that your spirit shall surge

With everlasting bliss and Gods own kiss

Towards eternal joy beyond matters of life

And that my friend is the sole objective of strife

So when I arrive, dishonour me not

Know that I mean all that's good

For through me you will find your true godly nature

Delusions will fade and the truth, you shall nurture.

Sensual Intoxication

Sensual Intoxication

With the precious gift of this life
I was blessed with senses five
Each one invaluable and priceless gems
From each my self worth stems
To be used with a sense of discrimination
Were meant to be used with love and compassion
Towards a life centric disposition.

My eyes, a gift to behold
The sight and vision, a window to the world
To see and admire the pristine universe's attire
See I did but with intent of greed
So it's you eyes who make me plunder
You are the cause of many a misdeed.

My ears that I hold so dear
Were to hear the heavenly melody and natures sounds
To hear a heartbeat or a raindrop, cooling the parched grounds
But what they like to hear, I am embarrassed to share
Vitrolius gossip that human folk tell
In that my eardrums joyfully revel
The sounds of distant guns, noisy traffic on a constant run
The slogans of violent lynch mobs
Those helpless women, their wails and sobs
Ears you must take the blame, for its absolutely your shame
You make me hear, acoustics of sadness and pain
Damn your antics and your total disdain.

And that one that sits haughtily on my face
For the breath of life, the nose you was made

Is lost in sensual fragrance and smells enchanting
Bodily scents and the wine intoxicating
Sweat smells bad but the blood odour is no more appalling
It shuns to inhale the cool forest air
Or the soothing aromas from the temples foyer
Such is your arrogance, you hold yourself so high
You cause me to falter and never tell me why.

Oh tongue, you are such a wicked witch
Up against my palate, you restlessly itch
For forbidden tastes, you lust and crave
The scotch and wine and that flesh tastes so fine
You don't rest there, your intent you nakedly bare
Most of all you relish the taste of blood
That from fellow beings, you shamelessly suck
But the words you utter are not any less bitter
Sometimes you sugarcoat your spoken content
Hiding the vanity and all that it represents
Your stark lethal words, hurt sharp like a knife
Killing many an affiliation, causing deep crevice
Ever changing your colours like a clever chameleon
You are truly unreliable, my malicious companion.

From the skin emanates, the sense of touch
And that's the one, I truly fear so much
Satin rich attires to velvety apparels
Your touch defines finesse and you want no other
But way beyond that, that feel you crave
The feel of flesh and my body you enslave
Lusty desires and smoldering fires
Gratify you must, by all means your carnal thirst
Imprisoning my being in physical chains

Reducing me to a body in its lesser domains.

Oh my senses you were meant to be divine

To make me a human with a grooming so fine

Alas I am held hostage, my mind and body is but a sensual cage

Much as I try, your iron grip to trim

I fail miserably and you mightily win

You potent five, you have held my life

To a devils ransom for which I must pay a heavy price

Price that shall atone me of your sins.

Free the soul I must and douse the hell within

And when I return to the creator of mine

I shall beg and pray

Don't give us humans the senses, they lead us astray

Instead infuse us at birth, with the fire of your holy hearth

So draw your sword and must you then slay

Senses your joy is short lived, there shall be a judgment day.

The invisible Chains

The Invisible Chains

From the dawn of mankind
That one chain that holds us in bind
That clips mans wings
So he may not soar or swing
Puts him in unseen fetters and confines
Takes away his freedom, imprisons his mind
It's the invisible hand that strangulates
Fear, is thy name that locks all gates.

Fear of uncertainty, fear of the unknown
Fear of authority, fear of the throne
Fear of failure, fear of hunger
Fear from thy neighbour, fear from the stranger
Fear from death all that we hold so dear
Fear from fear itself, no escape routes near
Fear in the mind, fear in the heart
Fear from oneself, it tears one apart.

A shadow, a constant companion in all that one does
It's a downward spiral, pulling down from above
Ruminations of the past, worries of the future
It entangles and blocks, the dreams one could nuture
Imaginary or true, its iron grip clutches you
And try as one may, it looks difficult to slay
Where fear thrives, there is no room for faith
It will steal your trust and bring blatant hate.

So slay it you must as soon as it strikes
Stare it in the face and stab it with a knife
And if it raises its ugly head again

Take a cudgel and strike with all your strength
So never look the other way or bend
Let your courage be your best friend
Like a knight in shining armour
Hold steadfast and never shall you flaunder.

Ignite a fire in the heart
Of great courage no matter what
For a fearless life is a life well lived
Fear fades away and faith is instilled
For tough times don't last but the tough ones do
Fearless are those souls and fearless must be you.

Ode to Death

Ode to Death

Oh death I say, you are such a faithful friend
You follow us beings to the very end
Your shadow travels with me everywhere
Many a times I know but do not care
From the day I was born you glanced at me in scorn.

You are not immortal so don't take pride
I shall be on watch and always by your side
Your invisible companion I shall see you grow
And when your time comes I shall let you know
With me to the divine home shall you go

As I fear and shudder, I try to utter
Death don't scare me I shall surely outsmart thee
I have the means to escape your clutches
You haven't yet seen all my riches
Health and life I can buy as I please
Immortal who knows but I shall not decease

You proud human let it be known that you are no God
You might have won the world and that's quite a lot
No doubt you have the ability to create what you have done
Space you have explored and on ocean bottoms you have run
Your science has moved beyond thinkable dimensions
Your technological creations are of unimaginable proportions.

But tell me human this one thing
Have you been able to create a living being
With a beating heart or eyes that sparkle

71

Or bring alive a dead man show me if you can
For if you do I am telling you
You shall be the master and death shall not anymore bother you
For if you cannot do this then accept the truth
Go down you must to the grave of dust
So against me you shall never win
Mortal you are and let that reality sink in.

Then as I see my tendrils grey fall upon my wrinkled face
That tells a story of a life's somber journey if one could trace
Eyes once so sparkling and blue can now see no more but a metres few
The steps are weary as I slowly stroll
The bygone years have taken their toll
As my chest heaves I know what death says is true
My breaths remaining are but a few
I have sung my song and it's time to bid adieu
But my heart is not yet ready to part
It cries in regret for things I could'nt get
And wants to hold on to dear life
But it has to wean and detach from the hive
To be able to go in peace and succor
And surrender to the kiss of death when it occurs.

Oh death let's make peace with each other
Upon your reality I deeply ponder
All my life in dread I despised you
Living a lie knowing it was'nt true
For you are the creators chariot divine
To bring us back home when it's our time
Let me love you as much as the life I have loved
For you are indeed life's beloved.
For what is life if there is no death

The frail body must be put to rest.

And the eternal soul must with the divine merge
For this dear death you give a gentle surge
Lifting one away from life's misery and pain
You take us where all stand to gain
Where eternal peace shall ever remain
So death let me welcome you when you arrive
Till then the gift of life I shall cherish and thrive.

The Oneness

'Myriad forms and yet one soul
Separate beings and yet whole
The miracle of oneness unfolds
For the one to see and behold.'

The Oneness of it All

The Oneness of it All

As I wake up to the morning sun
And the chirruping birds on my window sill
I pull the curtains, the sun rays enter in
The sight outside gives me a thrill
Majestic greens and the mountains yonder
What a heavenly sight to ponder
The rivulet caressing the rocks as it flows
Mixed hues shimmering and golden glows
The pristine waters and the wind that blows
The melodious strains as the leaves flutter
The musical hymns divine they utter.

The distant snows sparkle and shine
The hovering clouds decorate the skyline
The morning dew like pearls on the leaves
Dazzles and dances with the light breeze
As I open the door and step on the carpets green
The grass embraces my feet with a gentle gleam
The flowers grin, nodding their heads
Elated, as they dance on their earthen beds
On the branch of the Gulmohar tree
The hummingbird hums its songs of glee
Greet the day and take a bow
A bow to the cosmos, the universe divine
The dance of the oneness
A vision to behold.

The oneness that creates and destroys
The cycle of life with its immense joys
As I put my hands out to hug the oneness

I dissolve and merge

With the winds I surge

Up and up beyond the confines

To be a feather, a leave or a dazzling star

A twig, a flower, a bird or a stream gurgling afar

A lofty mountain, a running fountain

The great oak tree in all its splendor bloom

And that cloud chasing the golden moon.

That man or that woman

That child with the toy

Or the baboons on the branches

Chasing each other with squeals of joy

And as I dissolve and become one with the oneness

I cease to exist, all that exists is the oneness

The celestial soul that engulfs us all

In this oneness we live, and when time comes

Into this oneness we shall fall.

The Dance of Life

The Dance of Life

Behold, the pretty leaf, budding and green
Embraced by the branch, glowing in its sheen
It dances to the wind
Singing the songs of the breeze
In the spring of its life
Twirling in enormous delight
Life has just begun in all its grandeur
The leaf shines pristine and shows its splendour
How passionate is this youthful dance
With wind beneath the wings
And a devil's prance.

Come summer the leaf turns a tad yellow
But desiring to kiss the wind as it bellows
The fire is gone but the ambers burn
A gradual sway is all that can be done
Valiantly clinging to the branch
Holding on to dear life
Time has flown and the fall has arrived
The leaf turns crimson and a golden glow
Autumn leaves are falling slow
Covering the earth with their mortal hues
Winter beckons and soon trees shall be in blues.

Still the leaf clings on in unease
Rustling through the cool breeze
Alas the day arrives, a gale that blows strong
In the valley's heart, rips the leaf from the branch
Turning, tossing and tearing it apart
As the leaf rests on the breast of the earth

Soon to be one with it in spirit and soul
The gale is howling in all its might
And the snow make the grave on that winter night
And as the snows melt, the spring returns
Once again a leaf is budding on the branch.

Nursed by its mother, the tree of life
To blossom and grow, to dance and sing
With the sun and the blowing wind
To slowly wilt and then depart
To return to the earthen heart
The dance of the created and the creator continues
Creating, sustaining, destroying, it moves
The great mystery of life that none can decipher
So come, live and take what it has to offer.

Dance the dance and play the game
The game of life with its pleasure and pain
Sing the songs of a beating heart
That has lived through joys and sorrows
Through the yesterdays, today and tomorrows
Who are we, nothing but a leaf on the tree
For everything that is born must die in time
So dance as you return to your creator divine.

Existential Predicament

Existential Predicament

As I step into the winter of life
Having walked through the summer, autumn and spring
Day and night, a question rises and rings
In my heart and mind, a one of its kind
For who am I, I still don't know
In my twilight years, this bothers me so.

Alas my intellect so sharp I took tremendous pride in
Cannot decipher life and all that goes on within
My name, my religion, my success defined me
Me, mine, myself has been my world, the way I see.

My ego self sought to chase success and fame
For material accretion, I played many a unholy game
Each day the self, I made it strong
Making my own choices, right or wrong.

Having raced through life's maze as if it was all there was
But now the weary heart has hit a sudden pause
I have it all but why then the empty inner space
The nothingness of it stares starkly in my face.

As the lost consciousness of mortality sets in
A gloom descends and the senses go in a spin
The absolute truth hits me hard
Before long from this earth, I shall depart.

A burden of regret, guilt and self doubt
Who is the real me I never found out
Am I this perishable body and the mind

Or something much more
This query haunts me like never before.

Am I the soul that scriptures define
Or just an illusionary reflection in the mirage of time
Where did I come from, where will I go
My end is near, this anguish plagues me so.

And in the midst of all this delusion
Amongst hideous chaos and utter confusion
I turn to the unknown and it says 'just be'
Know you might not but you are a part of me

An eternal being in a human form
To live your existence, till I call you home
You were born of me and shall return to thee
Sing your song for you shall soon be free.

My desperation and despair as if by magic dispel
I feel deep peace and tranquil
As I bow in reverence and gratitude
I feel your blessing of fortitude
My mortality is the sacred path to the eternal
So my song I shall merrily sing, till life comes full circle.

Creator's Lament

Creator's Lament

Humans you, the creators own reflection

Believe you are the celestial conception

Superior to all, other species earthen

Higher than all other universal brethren

Inflated egos with pride you wear

With conceit and arrogance, your minds you smear

For material desires you damage and destroy

You even want what money can't buy

Cunningly you connive, to selfishly thrive

Craving for power, you hungrily strive.

Running in the rat race to outdo the other

Has sadly become your prime nature

By hook or by crook, you must reach the top

Till you succeed you must not stop

Success you measure by wealth and fame

For this you can play any foul game

The voice of your conscience you scuffled long ago

Your egoistic self drives you and there you go

Moral values oh you don't give a damn

The facade you put in public is nothing but a sham.

Sheer greed, not need is what you live by

Inequality and exclusion gives you great joy

If it serves you well, you create wide rifts

Between poverty of the spirit and soul you drift

Shallow to the core, you choose to ignore

Humility, love, and compassion you spurn

To anger, arrogance, hate you turn

Murder or rape, nothing repels you

Sadist or a bigot, you don't care a fig, do you
Humanity, what's that, don't try to preach
You have your own lessons to live by and teach.

Your intense yearning is to be nothing less than me, the God
Rule you must this world, be its pseudo lord
Immortal you are or that's what you think
You can make the world vanish with a nuclear blink
I made you from five elements from my own crust
But control them now you absolutely must
For supremacy, for wealth, for carnal satiation, you lust
To make hell out of heaven is the skill you have honed
Relentlessly uncontent, even nature you have conned.

Human I made you, the most higher of all species
But you used my divine gifts to shatter and hammer to pieces
This heavenly earthen home and the lesser life forms
You really own nothing yet you call everything your own
Your tremendous egos have created wars and famine
Bringing immense havoc to all creations mine
Have I created a devil or a Satan, I grimly wonder
My most cherished construct has turned a Frankenstein monster
As I fret and regret, I sadly ponder
My labour of love has turned out to be a blunder.

All I wanted from you was universal affection and compassion
Away from greed, anger and material obsession
To spread joy and imbibe my virtues divine
Sadly to which you didn't give a dime
But I your eternal father how can I disown you
Rebel, my spoilt child but I still love you
So internalize my spirit and free thyself

86

Of evil pursuits and pure selfishness

Find your soul within, which is nothing but me

A glittering spark, of divinity

Return to your home, the abode of the eternal

Return to what I made you, of pure consciousness and spiritual.

A Devil's Mourning

A Devil's Mourning

As I hurried across the woods with the twilight dwelling

Across the trees I heard the jackals yelling

No wind or even a gentle breeze

Everything seemed at great unease

Was it a lull before a fiery storm

For a November evening, it was rather warm

I scurried along in a hurry

As fast as my legs would carry

But suddenly I stopped dead on my trail

My eyes turned wide and my colour so pale.

Blocking my path was a demonic form

With bloodshot eyes and thorny horns

Who are you, I mustered some courage

As I looked at the creature, so brutal and savage

Laughing aloud, it barred its white teeth

And then in anger it seemed to seethe

Strange you don't know me, you fool

It's me you depend upon for your various tools

To perform the deeds that your ego self demands

You nudge me and awaken me to meet your commands.

To fetch you some anger and bring you some hate

You must attack the other before it's too late

And sprinkle some greed over and above all that you need

So you can be wealthy and show off your creed

Send you some conceit dressed in a sheep's clothes

So non can spot the wolf in you to loathe

And worse still show you the way to kill

But alas, your conscience, it bothers you still

So put a knife to its heart and tear it apart
You don't need its advice, you am not a novice
Fill you with contempt and cook up some scorn
Help you belittle all whom you spurn.
Do as I tell you for obey you, I must
Or you, my master shall turn me to dust.

But today my master, I can take it no more
So I have come to confront you, I'm the Devil you adore
But I have to say, dispute this if you may
For even though he is wicked and smart
 A Devil like me has a heart
You invoke me so brutally, it's taken a heavy toll
My body is bruised, my weary head rolls
Your evil nature has even surpassed mine
On others unhappiness you dance and dine.

You cause so much pain and that's your evil gain
I'm your partner in crime, I say with disdain
Tasks I don't like but you make me do
And even though I am the Devil, I despise humans like you
Today I have come to end it all
So from the cliff of your own doing, to death you shall fall
And me, I shall cling to you
As for my deeds, I need to die too
Saying this the Devil pulled me in his arms
And together hurled us off the cliff as I wailed in alarm.

The images from my life flashed before my teary eyes
Indeed I had done no good, I deserved to die
There was a God within me but I became the Devil's advocate
Never listening to my conscience, I choose rampant hate

As I descend into the hellish ravine

I pray human, listen to your conscious divine

For it shall grace you with sacred actions

And glide you to your higher self and liberation

Me in despair and deep regret I go

I befriended the Devil and the end must be so.

Thou Indiscernible One

Thou Indiscernible One

They say you don't exist, why then I see you everywhere
Down from the sky, the sun and the moon, you stare
Your breath is the wind, the one we breathe in
Lovingly, caressing and birthing anew
In the depths of the ocean and the morning dew.

They say you can't touch
Why then I feel your omnipresence
As you illuminated rays warm the earthen face
A feeling so intense I feel your grace
Deep inside as the heart beats, beneath the bony ribs
A surge of emotion, a song of devotion
Rises up to question, the cause of commotion
As your hand holds mine so tender
A touch that brings complete surrender
A gentle warm embrace, in your realm I place
My heart for it knows the precious life that you bestow.

They say you don't speak, why then I hear you sing
In the rustling breeze that flows with ease
In the gurgling stream, in the velvet carpets green
In the clouds and the thunder, in the waves splashing down under
In the tango of the trees, and the humming of the bees
From the church chimes, its sacred hymns
From the aarti and aazan, and the kirtan at dusk and dawn
In the laughter of a child, or a mothers gentle chide
Chirruping birds in daylight, insect cacophony in dark nights
And when the melody falls upon the ears
It sure does feel that you speak from near.

They say you don't listen, why then I think you do

In the silence between the breaths, I can feel you are there

When I raise my head to the skies,

You look down through your piercing blue eyes

When I bow down in prayer, your silent words dispel all fears

When in despair I am crying, you warmly cradle my being

Whenever in anguish I fall in distress

You carry me across and remove my stress

Away from the worldly sorrows, to a better tomorrow

On a dark stormy night, when nothing seems right,

In hope I kneel, your radiance soothes and heals.

When I put my hand to my heart beneath

It's you that flutters and it's you that beats

You the ultimate, the creator of mine

The existential truths you so mysteriously define

The answers to which science really has none

Of birth and deaths and how destinies are spun

For humans, we are our limited minds

Must travel beyond ourselves to reach you, the divine.

Like a Rudderless Boat

Like a Rudderless Boat

Who am I, am I or not
Where have I come from, where to I walk
I know not nothing, nothing is what I know
Whether I even exist, what identity should I show.

Then what is this, this body and mind
I have no answer, please help me find
Life is passing by but I don't know why
What am I looking for in this aimless sojourn
My feet falter but I am still on a run.

Who will give the answers, who will shed some light
Whom should I meet to discuss my plight
Should I leave and embrace the Himalayan snows
To meditate and for answers to know
Or should I immerse in the Ganges so blue
Or be a renunciated yogi, I have no clue.

Scattered is everything, shattered is my being
A mirage on the sands is all that I am seeing
The only thing I know is that I know nothing
No destination in sight but still I am going
On a lonely road, no end to this drift
I am surrounded by a haunting mist.

Difficult is the journey within but what is easy tell me
The life is spent in meaningless quandary
The day follows night and the night after day
Time is ever on the move and fleeting away
Neither in daylight nor in the darkness of night

Contentment and peace remains out of sight
Strange is this dilemma, a twin to me
Like a rudderless boat, adrift on the sea
Will it ever find the shore, doubts creep inside
The storm is engulfing me, I might sink with the tide.

Nothing is mine that is of worth to loose
Not even the shadow that one can choose
All things are at mercy of the mighty time
The breath and the beating heart of mine
The life you consider your own shall betray
Four moments and then it shall fade away.

So away from this self to the home of divine
To make this voyage, day and night I pine
To be away from the me, I approach lord thee
Oh Allah, let me in, have mercy on me
Pray, show me the path to my destiny.

If he clasps my wavering hand
And becomes an eternal friend
If he can pick up and dust this tainted heart
Ignite a flame within that never parts
Saves a drowning mortal, carry him ashore
What else could one want, is there anything more.

In hope I live and the path I walk
Not knowing anything for what do I really know
But that flickering light, it burns me so
So the arduous journey has begun, oh lighter of the lamp
In this lifetime or another, bestow thy grace so I may reach your camp.

Miracles

Miracles

What a wondrous day when is born the child
The birthing cries bring tears to her eyes
The mother she holds the infant on her bosom
A sight to behold the union of the twosome
Hot wet droplets she rains on the tiny head
If one sought a miracle here ends the quest
The timeless magic of creation witnessed at its best.

Outside above the skies have turned black
Raging the wind gallops on a horseback
A mighty gale confronts the dark cloud
Roaring thunder as the sounds grow loud
Downfalls from the sky the rain drops crying
Filling up lowlands that are slowly drying
The clouds well up large tears with love for their dear
The parched earth and its children would die they do fear.

So the twosome together, they make a mighty weather
And rain so hard that their tears strike the earthen heart
Till she can take in no more and with plenty to store
She sheds tears of joy spilling at every nook
Across the rivers and gurgling brook
Waterfalls that fall from dizzy heights
Fill the lakes shuddering in delight
If this is not magical then what is
Tell me someone is this not sheer bliss.

The earth romances and around him she dances
Flirting with the sun and sometimes with the moon
Her two aspiring suitors, they try their best to woo

But she spins with all her might, bringing the day and night
Half lit up and half dark, she's playful like a lark
And not to forget the seasons with hard toil she does bring
Come summer, then autumn, after winter and then spring
And the foursome bring a splash of colours that astound
Paint exquisite landscapes everywhere and all around
And if you have lived to witness this magnificent design
I'm telling you this, you have lived a life quite fine.

For what does the soul want from this life with its short span
To feel the daft of fresh air, the warmth of the sun
The love of Mother Nature, the bliss of being one
With all that astounds and completely surrounds
Each day a new miracle, each night an exquisite spectacle
The cosmos is creating, millions miracles in the making
Pray, watch with care, there is magic everywhere
So feel it my friend before it's too late
For time is ever running and there is a due date.

You are here for a reason, to witness every season
With awe and wonder, of the endless grandeur
The miracle of life and all that it brings
Its love and joy, its sorrow and stings
For if there is a beginning, there must also be an end
Mortal being unite with this magic, let your heart sing
And when the knight of death arrives, tell him lets go
To witness yet the biggest miracle with awe and grace
Of merging with the divine magician in his everlasting embrace.

Printed in Great Britain
by Amazon

16068061R00062